Call On The Lord
By Selena Millman

Call On The Lord
By Selena Millman

ISBN: 978-1-365-59499-1

Lyrics:

Seeking You, Lord
I Seek You, Lord
Thank You, Lord, For Loving Me
Cross In The Sky
Teach Me, Lord
Speak It
Before All
Call On The Lord
Please Guide Me
Why Don't People Believe In Jesus
Dear Jesus, Teach Me
O Lord, Please Show Me How
Praise The Lord
Jesus Says
Lessons From The Bible
I Know You Are There, Lord
I See The Jesus In You
Can You Hear Me, Lord
Lord, Why Love Me
Lord, Can You Light My Way
Create In Me
A New Heart
Here I Am, Lord

This book is connected to a few of my stories:

Running To Love
ISBN: 978-1-257-88066-9

Heroic Love
ISBN: 978-1-257-92611-4

and

Spirit Of Love
ISBN: 978-1-105-19833-5

Plus Cherished Love
(Not published yet - the one after Accepting Love - ISBN:
978-1-365-41754-2)

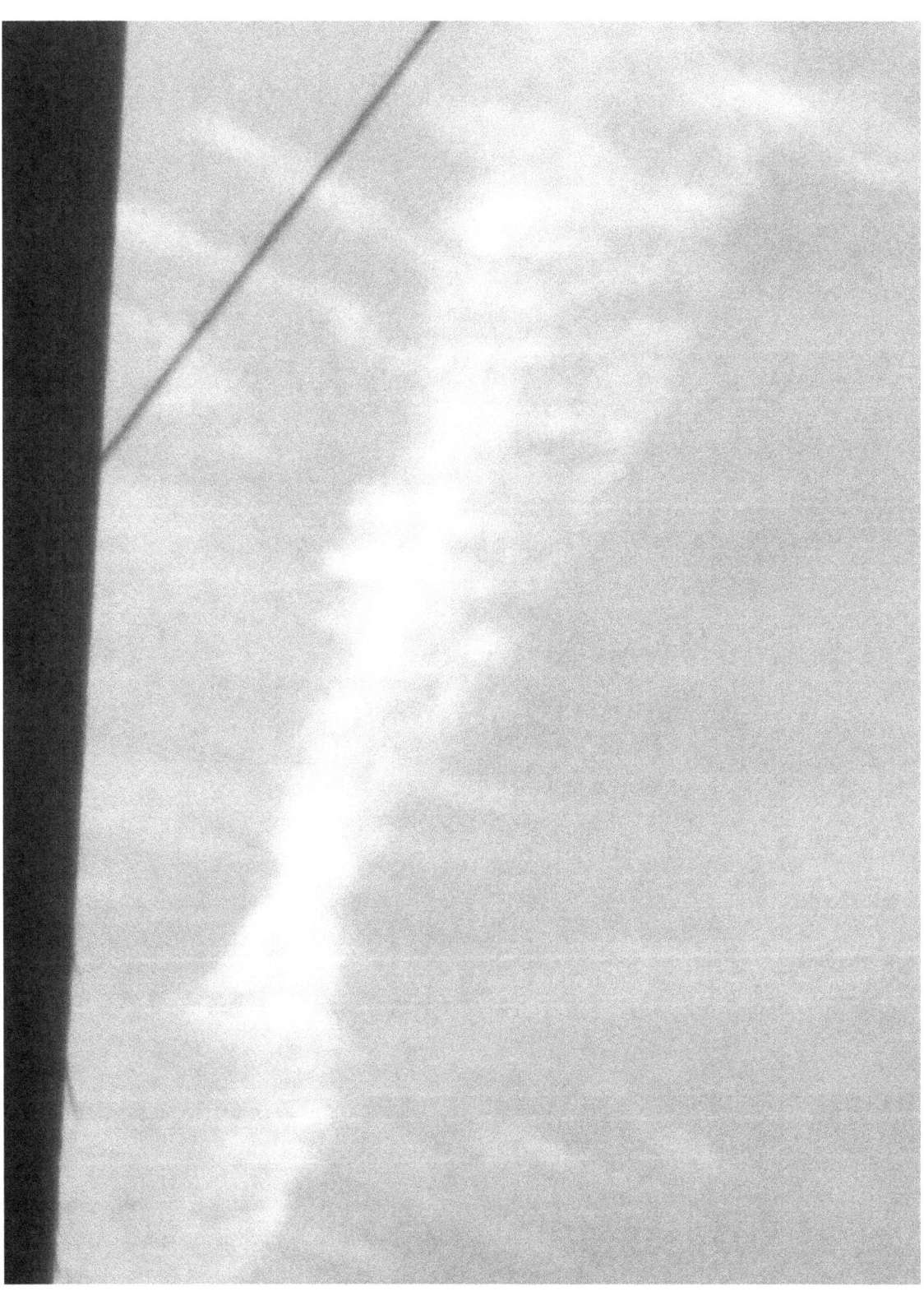

Seeking You, Lord

Written by Selena Millman
Written on November 6, 2011

Chorus:

Seeking You, Lord
Studying Your Word every day
Learning more and more
Fill me with Your Spirit, dear Lord
God, my Heavenly Father
Jesus, my Heavenly Brother
I love thee so

Verse:

Teach me
Guide me
Show me Your way
Let me be humble

Chorus:

Seeking You, Lord
Studying Your Word every day
Learning more and more
Fill me with Your Spirit, dear Lord
God, my Heavenly Father
Jesus, my Heavenly Brother
I love thee so

Verse:

I cast my worries on You
Let me walk with You
Show me the way, dear Lord
Help me forgive
Those I need to forgive

Chorus:

Seeking You, Lord
Studying Your Word every day
Learning more and more
Fill me with Your Spirit, dear Lord
God, my Heavenly Father
Jesus, my Heavenly Brother

I love thee so

Verse:

Allow me to shine
Your Love on this world
I want to be a good example
I want to learn Your ways
I want to know You, dear Lord

Chorus:

Seeking You, Lord
Studying Your Word every day
Learning more and more
Fill me with Your Spirit, dear Lord
God, my Heavenly Father
Jesus, my Heavenly Brother
I love thee so

Verse:

If it be Your will
Shine a Blessing on me
Thank You Lord

I Seek You, Lord

Written by Selena Millman
November 2016

Verse:

Woke up with my mind fixed on You
Had You on my mind all day

Chorus:

Early in the morning
Through the day
And late at night
Will I seek You, Lord

Verse:

Raining outside
Clouds are grey
That's not dampening my spirits
My heart is full of Praise

Lift Him up
Lift up the Lord

I meditate on Your Law day and night

Chorus:

Early in the morning
Through the day
And late at night
Will I seek You, Lord

Verse:

I need more of You, Lord
And less of me

Thank You for saving me
I can't thank You enough

I will Praise You every day
And every night too

Chorus:

Early in the morning
Through the day
And late at night
Will I seek You, Lord

Verse:

I Love You, Lord
And I won't take that back

Thank You, Lord, For Loving Me

Written by Selena Millman
Written on November 6, 2011

Chorus:

Thank You, Lord, for loving me
Thank You for giving me life
Thank You for waking me up this morning
Again, I say thank You, dear Lord

Verse:

Your Hand is in everything
Your wonderful Hand
Every good thing comes from You
Thank You for safety
You protect me every day
Even when I don't realize it
I know You do

Chorus:

Thank You, Lord, for loving me
Thank You for giving me life
Thank You for waking me up this morning
Again, I say thank You, dear Lord

Verse:

You woke me up
When You didn't have to
You bless me every day
You blessed me with life
I'm still here
Thanks to You

Chorus:

Thank You, Lord, for loving me
Thank You for giving me life
Thank You for waking me up this morning
Again, I say thank You, dear Lord
Thank You so much my Lord

Cross In The Sky
Written by Selena Millman
Written November 2016

Verse:

The Lord is always there
The Lord is always good

Chorus:

Cross in the sky
Among the clouds
A sign from God
Jesus is Real
Holy Spirit is Leading

Verse:

Alone in my room
Drowning in tears
The Lord is there

Oh taste and see that the LORD is good.
Blessed is the man who takes refuge in him.

Chorus:

Cross in the sky
Among the clouds
A sign from God
Jesus is Real
Holy Spirit is Leading

Verse:

I look out my apartment window
I see a sight
A glorious sight
A Cross among the clouds

Does anyone else see the Cross?
Is it a sign for me?
Is it a reminder?

Chorus:

Cross in the sky
Among the clouds
A sign from God
Jesus is Real
Holy Spirit is Leading

Verse:

A sign of Love for me to see
Assurance from my Lord and Savior

Lord, thank You for letting me see
The Cross in the sky

Scripture mentioned: Psalm 34:8 (from the World Messianic
Bible)

Teach Me, Lord
Written by Selena Millman
November 2016

Chorus:

Show me your ways, LORD.
Teach me your paths.
Guide me in your truth, and teach me,
For you are the God of my salvation,
I wait for you all day long.

Teach me your way, LORD.
I will walk in your truth.

Verse:

I want to be humble
Help me be humble

Teach me, Lord
Help me learn and obey

Chorus:

Show me your ways, LORD.
Teach me your paths.
Guide me in your truth, and teach me,
For you are the God of my salvation,
I wait for you all day long.

Teach me your way, LORD.
I will walk in your truth.

Verse:

Help me endure

Help me cast my cares on You
And not take it back

Help me focus
Help me grow in faith
Help me access Your Peace

Chorus:

Show me your ways, LORD.
Teach me your paths.
Guide me in your truth, and teach me,
For you are the God of my salvation,
I wait for you all day long.

Teach me your way, LORD.
I will walk in your truth.

Verse:

Let me be an intercessor
Help me know who to pray for

I want to help someone
Let me help and heal

Let me be a blessing for someone

Scripture mentioned: Psalm 25:4-5 and Psalm 86:11 (from the
World Messianic Bible)

Speak It

Written by Selena Millman
November 2016

Chorus:

It's not enough to believe
You have to speak it
You have to say it

Verse:

that if you will confess with your mouth that Jesus is
Lord, and believe in your heart that God raised him from
the dead, you will be saved.
For with the heart, one believes resulting in
righteousness; and with the mouth confession is made
resulting in salvation.
For, "Whoever will call on the name of the Lord will be
saved."

Let the world know Jesus is the Son of God
Jesus is King of kings and Lord of lords

Jesus is Real
He really came in the flesh
He came to save us

Chorus:

It's not enough to believe
You have to speak it
You have to say it

Verse:

Believe in your heart
Then confess with your mouth

Believe
Then say what you believe

Scripture mentioned: Romans 10:9-10, 13 (from the World
English Bible)

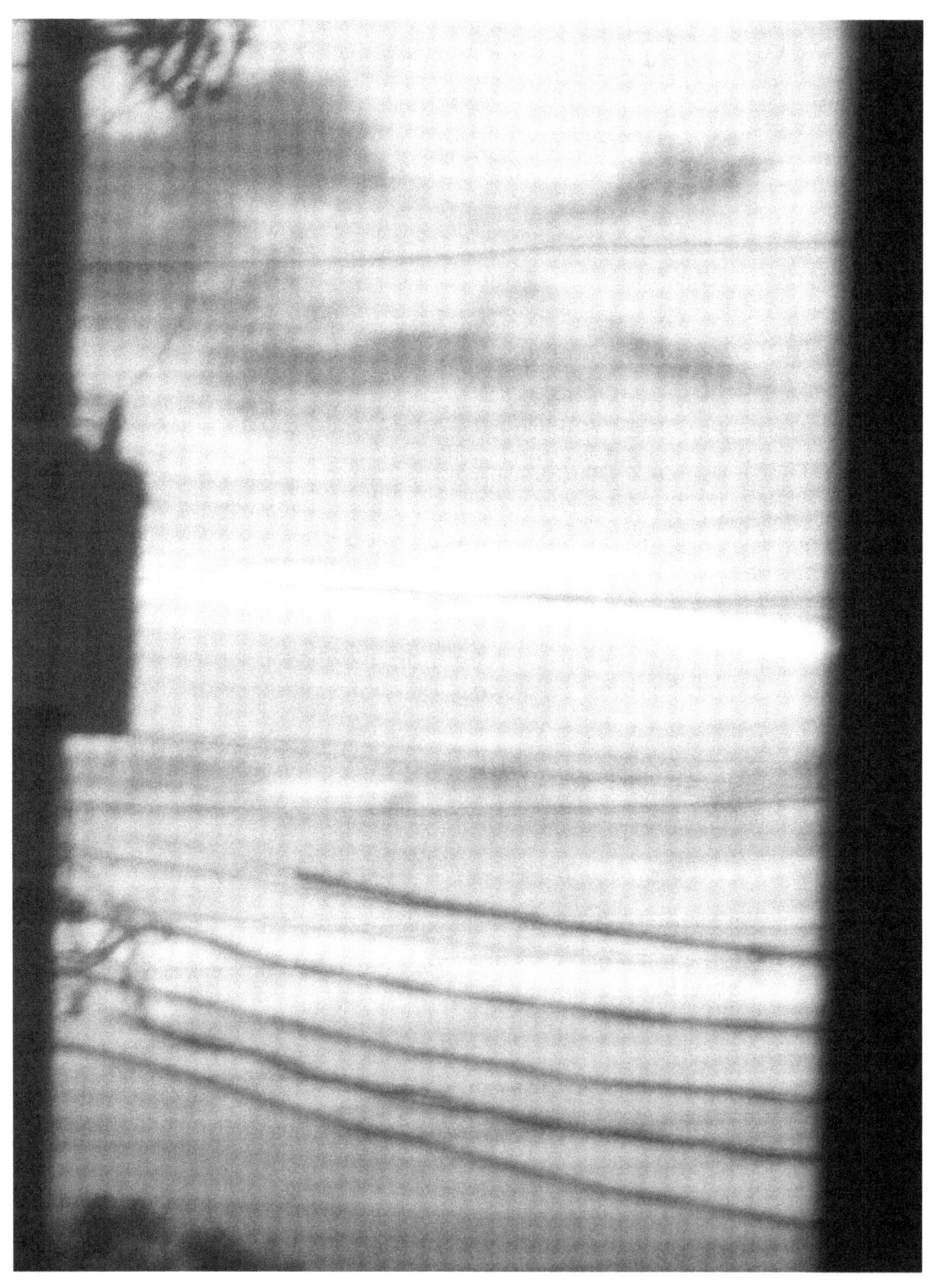

Before All
Written By Selena Millman

Chorus:

In the beginning, God created the heavens and the earth.

By wisdom the LORD founded the earth.
By understanding, he established the heavens.
By his knowledge, the depths were broken up,
and the skies drop down the dew.

Verse:

Before the water and the land
Before the animals
Before the world
You were there

You created all
You are everywhere
You see all and know all

Chorus:

In the beginning, God created the heavens and the earth.

By wisdom the LORD founded the earth.
By understanding, he established the heavens.
By his knowledge, the depths were broken up,
and the skies drop down the dew.

Verse:

Thank You for giving me life
Thank You for Your Mercy

Thank You for another day

Scripture mentioned: Genesis 1:3 and Proverbs 3:19-20
(World Messianic Bible)

Call On The Lord

Written By Selena Millman
December 2016

Chorus:

Call on the Lord
Any day and any time
Remember the Lord is near
Don't forget Him

Verse:

Shout to the Lord
Praise His Name

Heavenly Father
I thank You every day
And every night

Chorus:

Call on the Lord
Any day and any time
Remember the Lord is near
Don't forget Him

Verse:

Jesus is in my heart
Jesus is in my thoughts
Jesus is in my life

I am so thankful I believe

Chorus:

Call on the Lord
Any day and any time
Remember the Lord is near
Don't forget Him

Verse:

Fill me, Holy Spirit
Lead me and teach me

Guide me through each day

Chorus:

Call on the Lord
Any day and any time
Remember the Lord is near
Don't forget Him

Verse:

I lift You up, oh Lord

Thank You for choosing me

Please Guide Me
Written by Selena Millman
November 2016

Verse:

Seeking You, Lord
Studying Your Word every day

I cast my worries on You
Let me walk with You
Show me the way

Chorus:

I want to be a good example
I want to learn Your ways
I want to know You

Verse:

Please fill me with Your Spirit

I want to live as You would

Please help me walk in Faith
I want to walk in Your ways
Please show me how

Chorus:

I want to be a good example
I want to learn Your ways
I want to know You

Verse:

Please teach me how, my Lord
Please guide me on my path to You

(written in character view for Nick)

Why Don't People Believe In Jesus
Written by Selena Millman
Written on November 6, 2011

Chorus:

Why don't people believe in Jesus
Can't you see He came from God
Isn't it obvious

Verse:

He did wonderful things
He performed miracles

Chorus:

Why don't people believe in Jesus
Can't you see He came from God
Isn't it obvious

Verse:

Surely He came from God
Surely He is God's Son

Chorus:

Why don't people believe in Jesus
Can't you see He came from God
Isn't it obvious

Verse:

He died to save us
And you can't even believe in Him
Why can't you

(Written in Character View (Nick) for Healing Love)

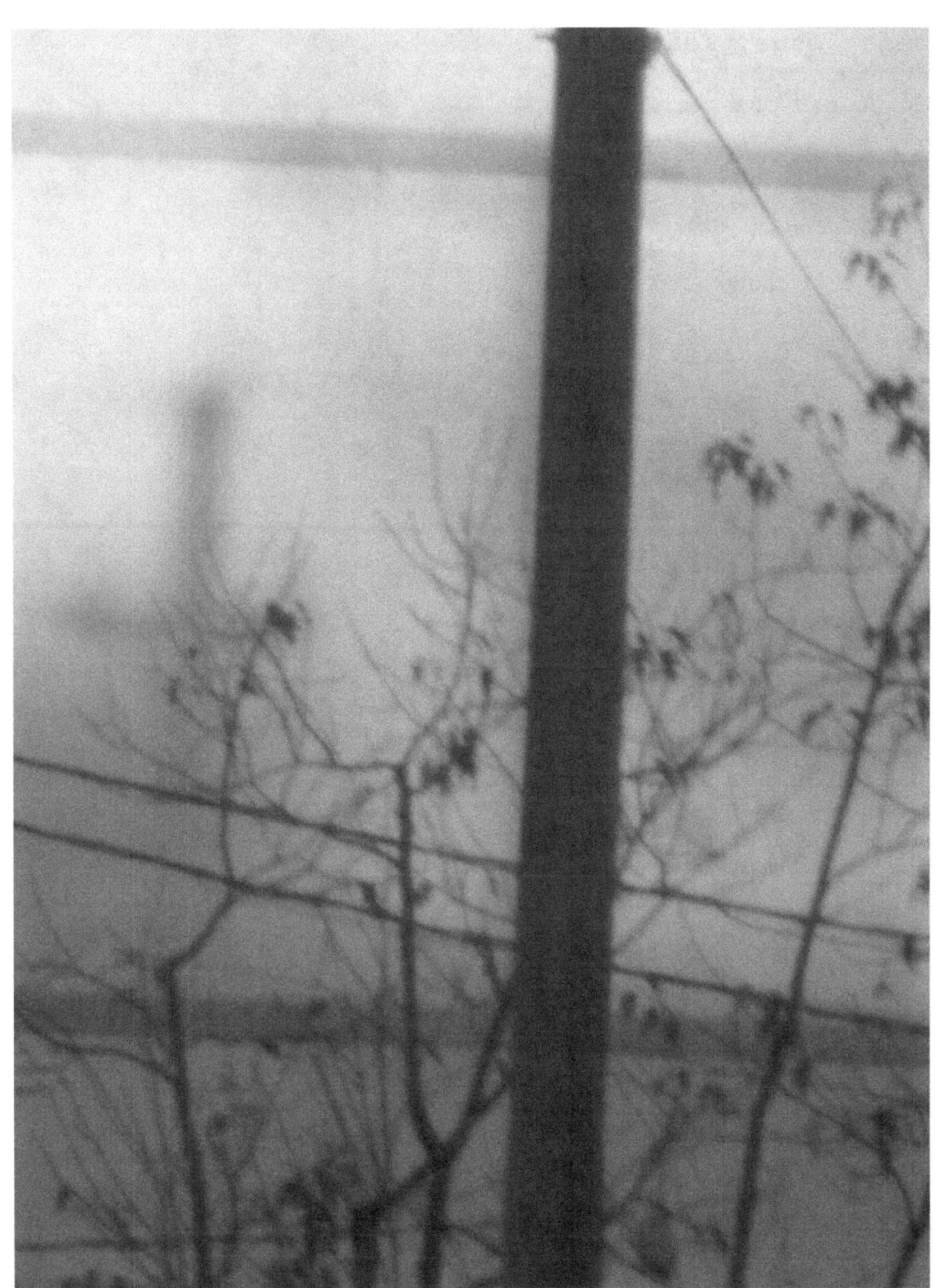

Dear Jesus, Teach Me

Written by Selena Millman
Written September 25th, 2011

Chorus:

I want to be like You, dear Jesus
I want to live like You did
I want to love like You do

Verse:

Dear Jesus, please teach me
Teach me to love like You do
Teach me to be strong
To be brave and full of faith
Dear Jesus, teach me to be wise
I want to know all You do

Chorus:

I want to be like You, dear Jesus
I want to live like You did
I want to love like You do

Verse:

Dear Jesus, teach me all You command
I want to learn everything
I aim to do as You say

Chorus:

I want to be like You, dear Jesus
I want to live like You did
I want to love like You do

Verse:

Please teach me, dear Jesus

(Written in Character View for Nick in "Spirit Of Love")

O Lord, Please Show Me How

Written by Selena Millman
Written July 17, 2011

Verse:

There is so much
I don't understand
I want to grow
I want to learn

Chorus:

O Lord, please show me how
Open my eyes and my mind
Open my heart to Your ways

Verse:

Our Heavenly Father is watching
He is in everything and is everywhere
Only believe what you can see
Then open your eyes to see

Chorus:

O Lord, please show me how
Open my eyes and my mind
Open my heart to Your ways

Verse:

I want to love like Jesus
He taught us to do right
What would Jesus do
I want to learn that
I want to learn more

Chorus:

O Lord, please show me how
Open my eyes and my mind
Open my heart to Your ways
Lord, please teach me

(Written in Character View for Nick in "Heroic Love")

Praise The Lord
Written by Selena Millman
Written September 25th, 2011

Chorus:

Praise the Lord
Praise His name
Say it with pride
He loves you so love Him back

Verse:

All good things come from God
We all sin
Saying otherwise is a lie
Confess to be forgiven

Chorus:

Praise the Lord
Praise His name
Say it with pride
He loves you so love Him back

Verse:

Pray sincerely
Be faithful

Chorus:

Praise the Lord
Praise His name
Say it with pride
He loves you so love Him back

Verse:

The Lord teaches us a lot
If we just pay attention
Our Heavenly Father is with us always
Nothing is impossible with God on your side
If you believe
God will protect you

(Written in Character View for Nick in "Spirit Of Love")

Jesus Says

Written by Selena Millman
Written September 25th, 2011

Chorus:

Jesus says to love each other
That is His command
This is what Jesus says
I know so because the Bible says so

Verse:

Be devoted
Live in peace
Do not seek revenge
Be humble
Do not be proud

Chorus:

Jesus says to love each other
That is His command
This is what Jesus says
I know so because the Bible says so

Verse:

Jesus is wise
Like our Heavenly Father
Jesus strengthens us
He is there in our times of need

Chorus:

Jesus says to love each other
That is His command
This is what Jesus says
I know so because the Bible says so

Verse:

Seek Jesus and you will find Him
He came to save us so give Him your heart

(Written in Character View for Nick in "Spirit Of Love")

Lessons From The Bible

Written by Selena Millman
Written September 25th, 2011

Chorus:

The Bible teaches many things
But you have to read and pay attention
Our Heavenly Father loves you
Jesus does too

Verse:

Love each other
Don't judge one another
It isn't our place to judge
Be humble
Pride comes before the fall

Chorus:

The Bible teaches many things
But you have to read and pay attention
Our Heavenly Father loves you
Jesus does too

Verse:

You have to believe in Jesus
To have eternal life
Love with a sincere heart
Don't be wicked
Love the Lord
And love Jesus
They are our family

(Written in Character View for Nick in "Spirit Of Love")

I Know You Are There, Lord
Written by Selena Millman
Written on December 29th, 2011

Verse:

Once I was in darkness
I thought I was alone

Now I know I'm never alone
Because You are always there

In my darkest hours
I know You are there

The Lord loves me
He will never leave me
He will never forsake me

Chorus:

I believe in the Lord
I will never stop loving Him

I believe in Jesus
I will never stop loving Him

Verse:

Nothing is too hard for the Lord
He sees all and knows all

He does not promise an easy life
He does not promise a life with no heartache

Believe in Him and He will come to you
He will hear your prayers and He will help you

Just because you do not see Him
Does not mean He is not there

Chorus:

I believe in the Lord
I will never stop loving Him

I believe in Jesus

I will never stop loving Him

Verse:

I love You, Lord
Thank You for loving me

I believe in You, Lord
I believe in You, Jesus

I trust You
And in You

I know You are there, Lord

(written in character <Nick> for Healing Love)

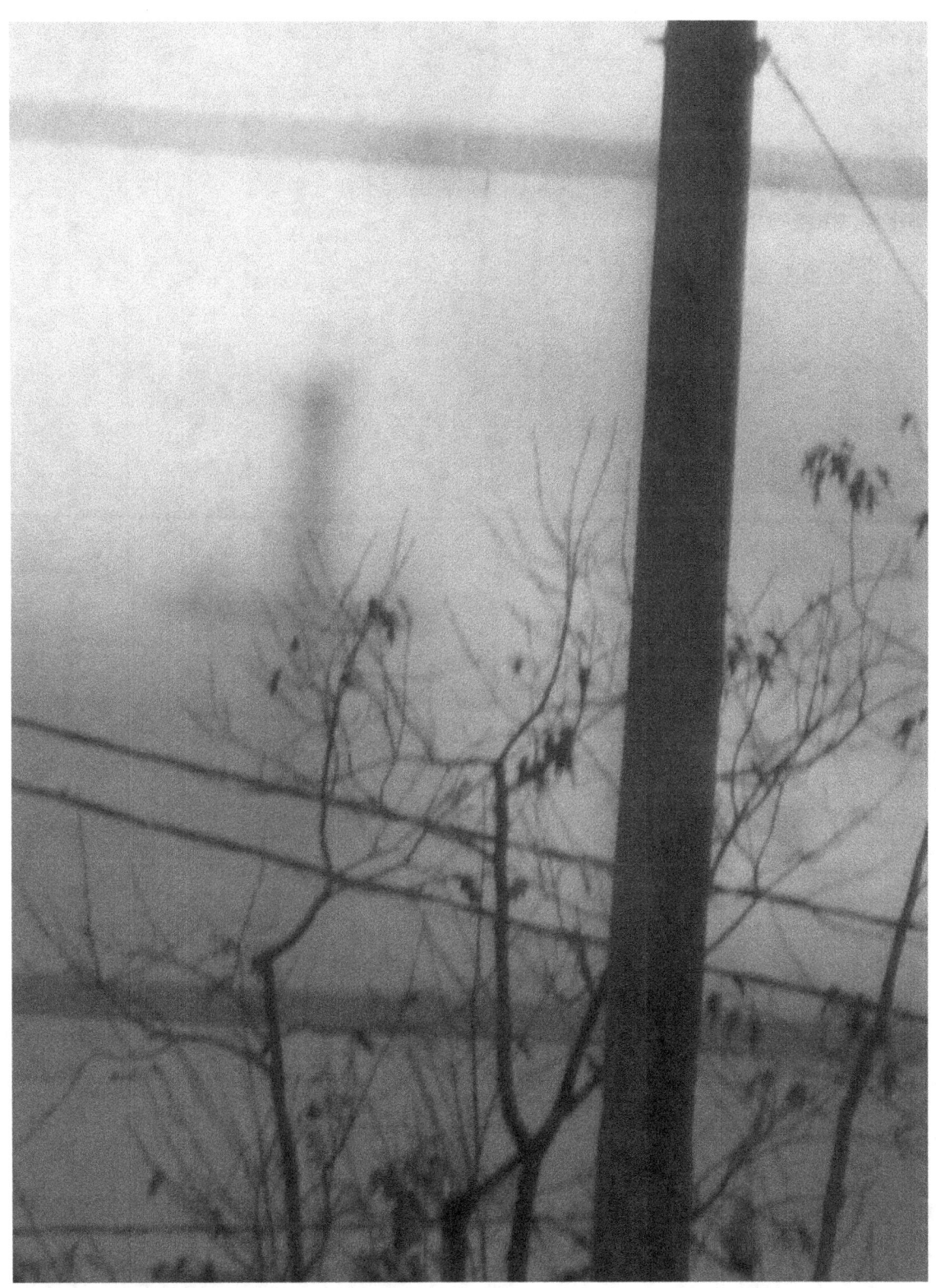

I See The Jesus In You

Written by Selena Millman
Written on December 29th, 2011

Verse:

My brother, you are so down on yourself
But I see you more clearly

You are humble
You guide me
You never leave me

Chorus:

I see the Jesus in you
He shines through you

You don't see it
But I do

Verse:

You'd even give your life for me
But please don't do that

You teach not to judge
Just like Jesus teaches

Chorus:

I see the Jesus in you
He shines through you

You don't see it
But I do

Verse:

You're all about love
You help so many

Just like Jesus

(written in character <Nick> for Healing Love)

Can You Hear Me, Lord

Written by Selena Millman
Written October 14 2011

Verse:

When I was a child
I was caught up in me
As an adult, can't say I'm much better

Never knew You were out there
Never even had a clue

Chorus:

Lord, are You watching
Lord, are You listening
Can You hear me, Lord

Verse:

Have You watched me through the years
Tell me, Lord
Did You cry as I cried
Please hear me, Lord

You have seen it all
At least that's what they tell me

Do You hear all I say
Do You know all I think
Is it so, Lord

Chorus:

Lord, are You watching
Lord, are You listening
Can You hear me, Lord

Verse:

I'm crying out loud
I've realized I can't do it alone

I'm reaching out
Will You reach back
Am I worthy

Chorus:

Lord, are You watching
Lord, are You listening
Can You hear me, Lord

(inspired by my character Ty for Healing Love)

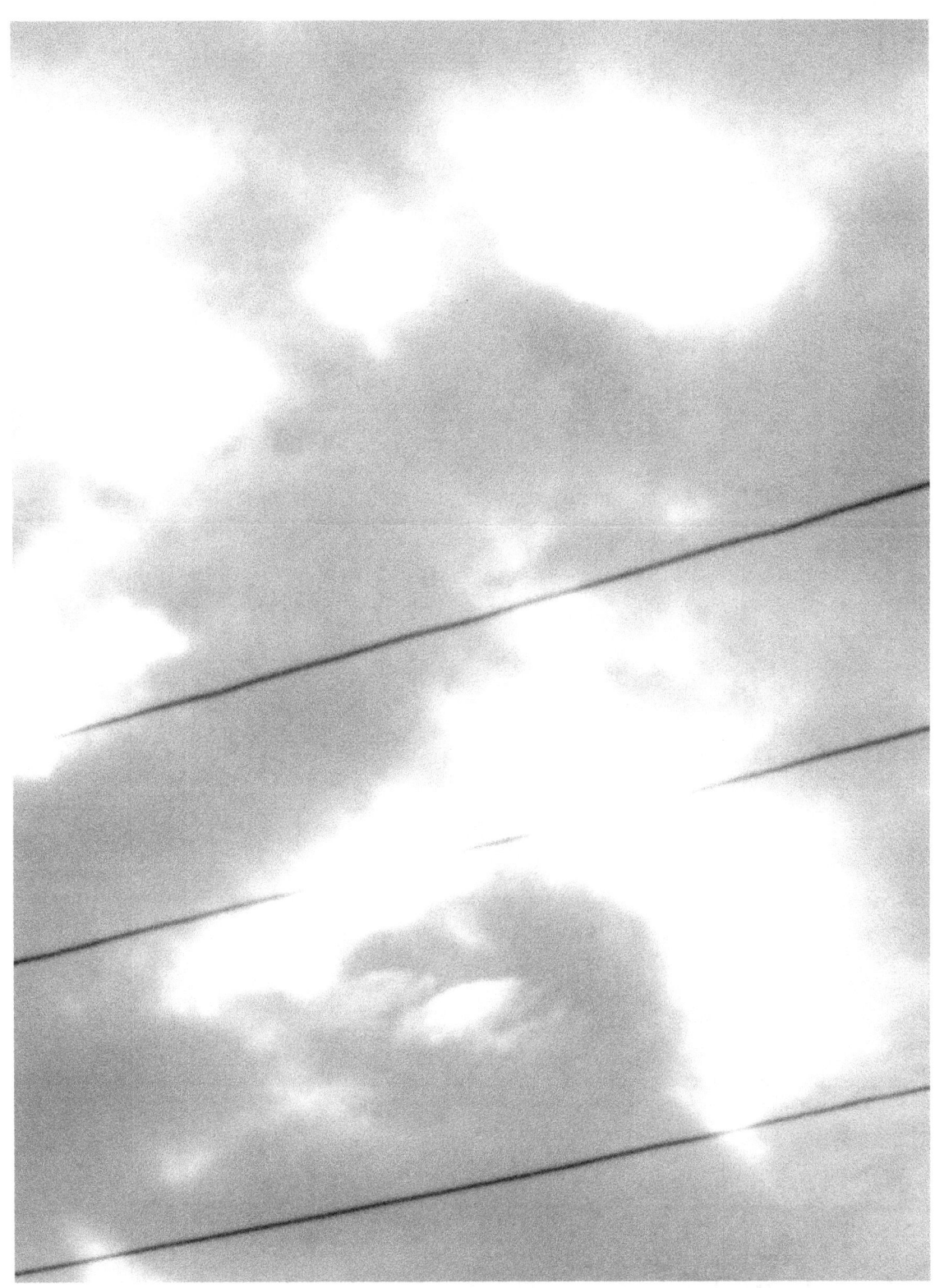

Lord, Why Love Me
Written by Selena Millman
Written in September 2011

Chorus:

You walk with me
Unseen You are there
In my darkest hours
And in my greatest joy
You still love me

Verse:

Why love me
I am not worthy
Heavenly Father
Jesus too
What do You see in me

Chorus:

You walk with me
Unseen You are there
In my darkest hours
And in my greatest joy
You still love me

Verse:

I've sinned all my life
I'm no better than anyone else
Why would You love me
You knew me before they did
Even before I was born
You know everything about me
I am unworthy yet

Chorus:

You walk with me
Unseen You are there
In my darkest hours
And in my greatest joy
You still love me

(Written in Character View for Ty in "Spirit Of Love")

Lord, Can You Light My Way
Written by Selena Millman
Written July 1, 2011

Verse:

Spent my life in darkness
Never seeing the light
Never even knowing it was there

Chorus:

God, if You are watching
Maybe send a blessing my way
People say You are always there
Lord, can You light my way

Verse:

Never knowing You
Never knowing You cared

Chorus:

God, if You are watching
Maybe send a blessing my way
People say You are always there
Lord, can You light my way

Verse:

Children introduced me to You
Now I see You are there
Now I see You are all around
You are there in the day
And stay through the night
God, if You can love a no one like me
Then I thank You for every day

Chorus:

God, if You are watching
Maybe send a blessing my way
People say You are always there
Lord, can You light my way

(Written in Character View for Ty in "Running To Love")

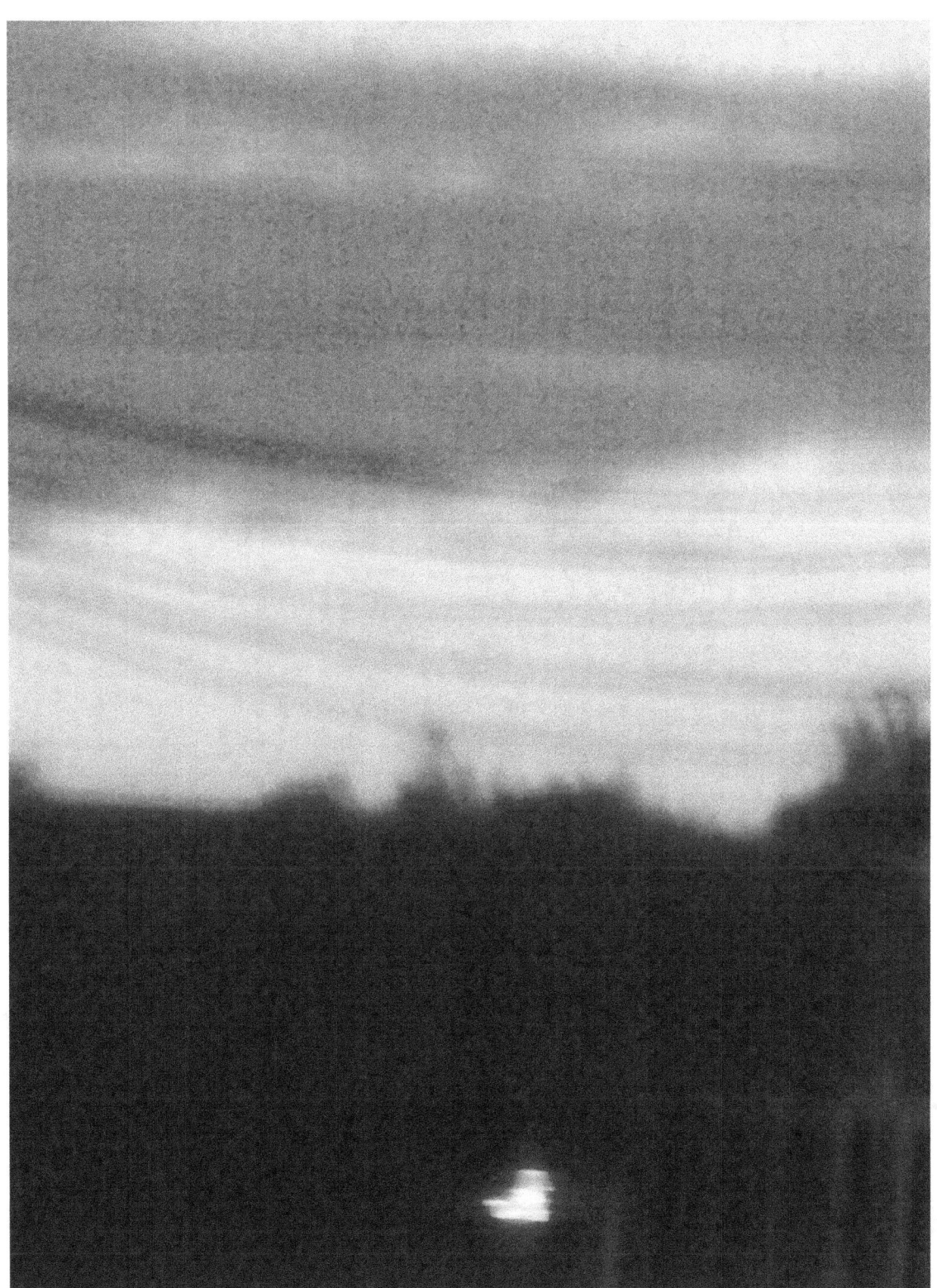

Create In Me
Written by Selena Millman
November 2016

Verse:

All I've seen
All I've said
All I've done

Chorus:

For I know my transgressions.
My sin is constantly before me.

Create in me a clean heart, O God.
Renew a right spirit within me.

Verse:

Pain is still in my heart
Help me break free
I can't do it on my own

Wouldn't have thought it possible
Thought I was too far gone

You brought Love into my life
You shined Light on the shadows in my life

Chorus:

For I know my transgressions.
My sin is constantly before me.

Create in me a clean heart, O God.
Renew a right spirit within me.

Verse:

Erase my doubt
Help me believe

Help me trust
Increase my Faith
I want to trust You

For so long it's been all pain
Help me cast my cares and not take it back

Chorus:

For I know my transgressions.
My sin is constantly before me.

Create in me a clean heart, O God.
Renew a right spirit within me.

Verse:

The clouds are lifting
I see the sun breaking through

(written in character view for Ty)

Scripture mentioned: Psalm 51:3, 10 (from the World English
Bible)

A New Heart
Written by Selena Millman
November 2016

Verse:

I'm many things
But don't let me be a hypocrite

Teach me how to put You first

Chorus:

I need a new heart
A fresh start
I need a new perspective

Verse:

Draw me in
Never let me go

Teach me Your Ways
And help me live by them

I can't save myself
I need You to save me

Chorus:

I need a new heart
A fresh start
I need a new perspective

Verse:

Darkness surrounds my past
It overwhelms my thoughts
I need Your Light to break through

Help me let it go
And focus on You

You know where I've been
You know where I'm going

I couldn't have made it without You

Chorus:

I need a new heart
A fresh start
I need a new perspective

Verse:

You watched over and protected me
Before I knew You

Chorus:

I need a new heart
A fresh start
I need a new perspective

(written in character view for Ty)

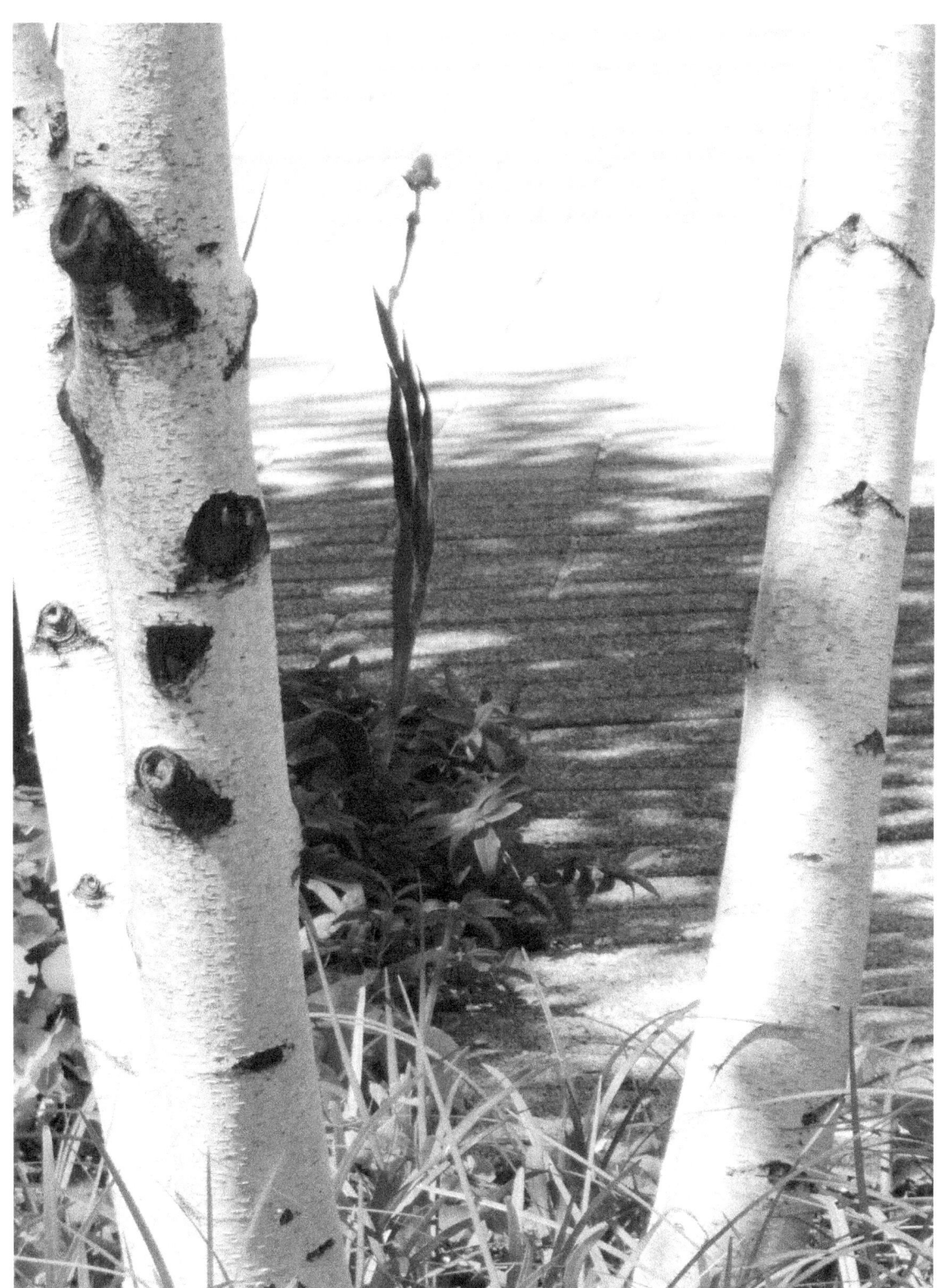

Here I Am, Lord

Written by Selena Millman
November 2016

Verse:

I am Your servant, Lord
Lead me and guide me
Let me know what You want me to do

Chorus:

Let me be strong in my faith
Faithful in my witness
Let my life be my testimony

Verse:

Help me be bold in proclaiming
Let me spread knowledge of You
And lead others to You

Chorus:

Let me be strong in my faith
Faithful in my witness
Let my life be my testimony

Verse:

I am not ashamed of the Gospel
I am thankful I believe in Jesus
I confess Jesus as Lord and Savior

I'm not afraid to proclaim Your Name
I'll shout Jesus so all can hear

Chorus:

Let me be strong in my faith
Faithful in my witness
Let my life be my testimony

Verse:

Let me be a good witness
Let my life testify

Let me stay faithful

Chorus:

Let me be strong in my faith
Faithful in my witness
Let my life be my testimony

Verse:

I am Your vessel, Lord
Mold me to how You want me to be

Here I am, Lord
Use me
Send me

(written in character view for Jye)

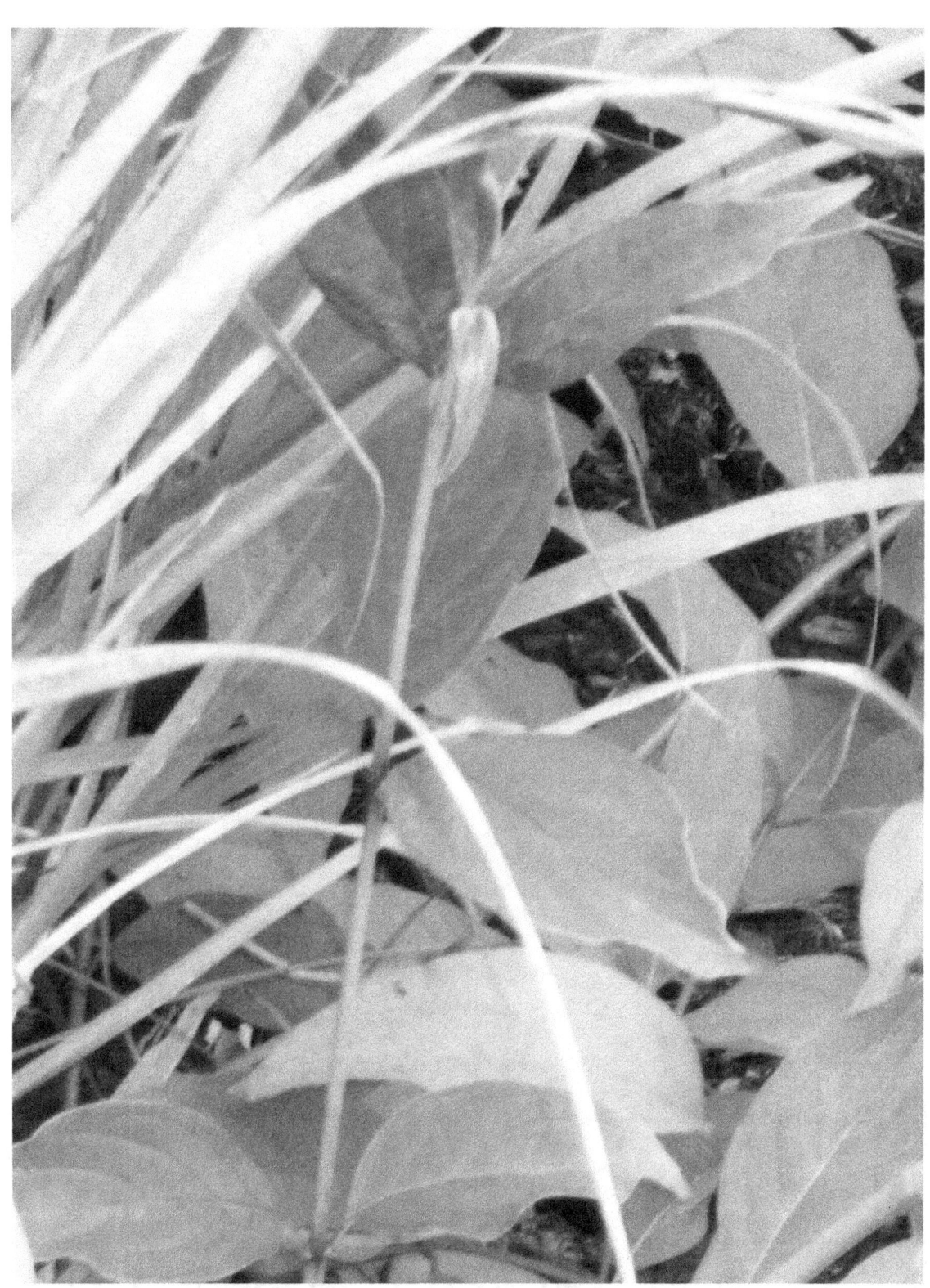

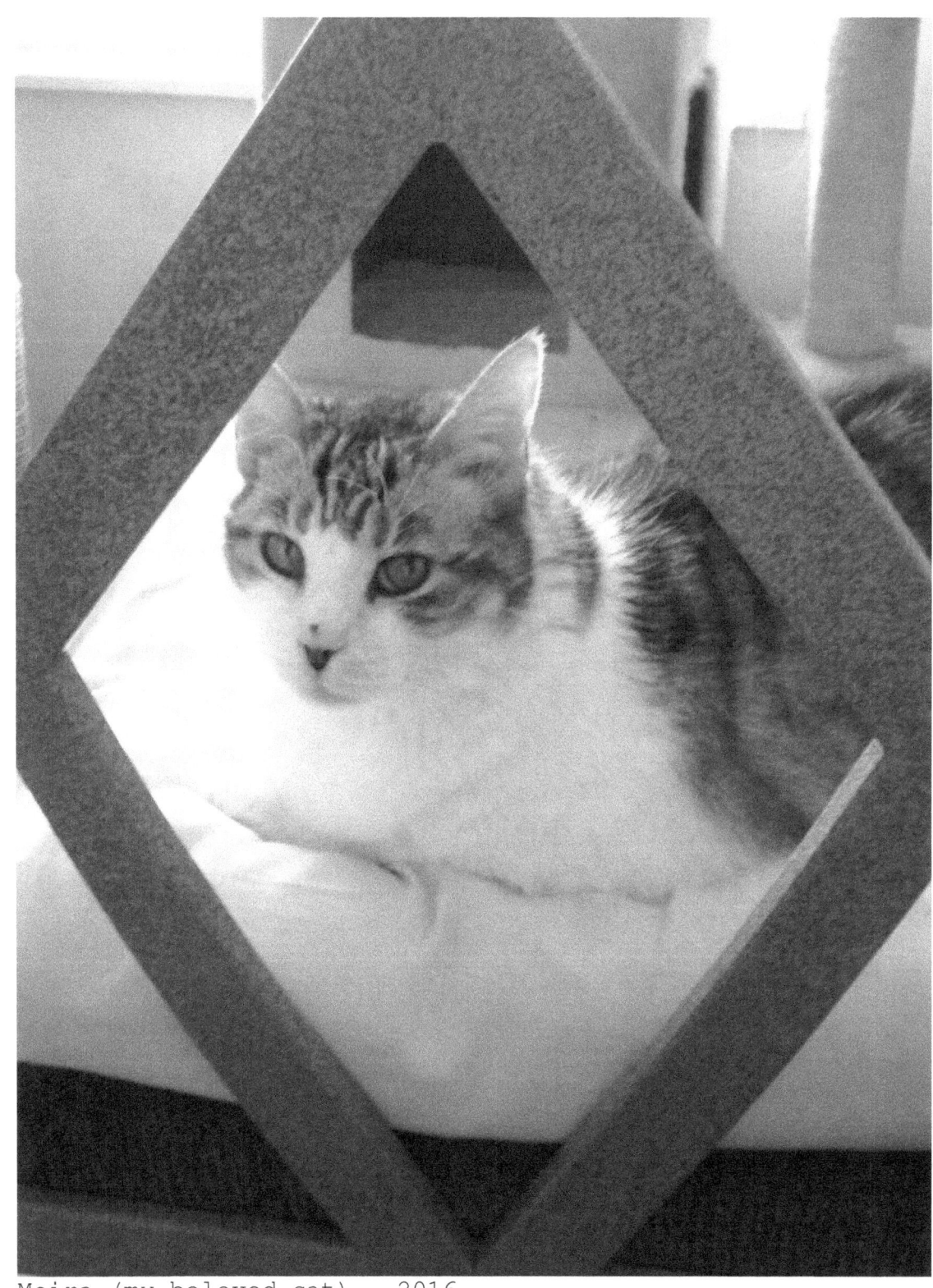

Moira (my beloved cat) - 2016

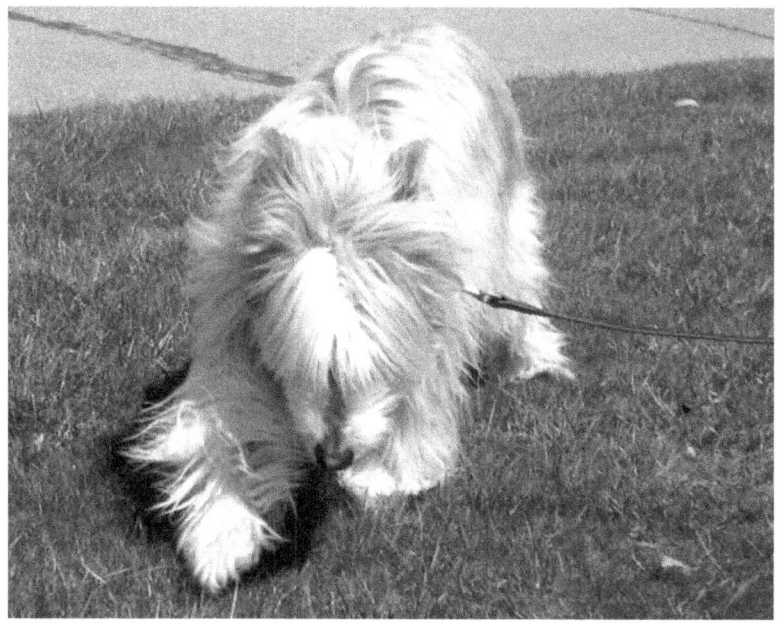

Tyler

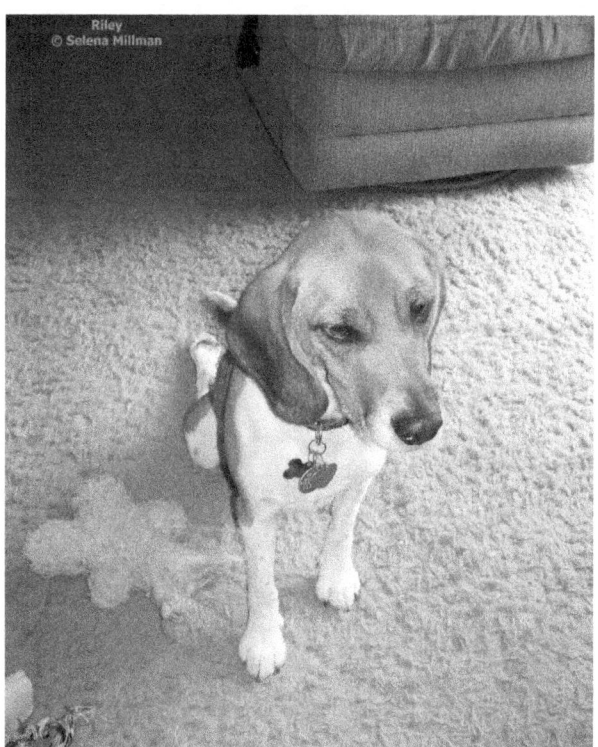

Riley

Scripture Mentioned:

Psalm 34:8
Psalm 25:4-5
Psalm 86:11
Romans 10:9-10, 13
Genesis 1:3
Proverbs 3:19-20
Psalm 51:3, 10

All Scripture is the World English Bible or the World Messianic Bible because they are the only two that are completely Public Domain.

Buy my Books and Photos at
http://www.lulu.com/heal4michael

Search Selena Millman at
http://www.amazon.com

My Devotional Pages:
(Sermon Notes, Scripture, and Devotions)
http://heart4jesus.webs.com/
http://loveforjesus.webs.com/

My Books:
http://booksbyselena.webs.com/

Creative Page:
http://all4ty.webs.com/

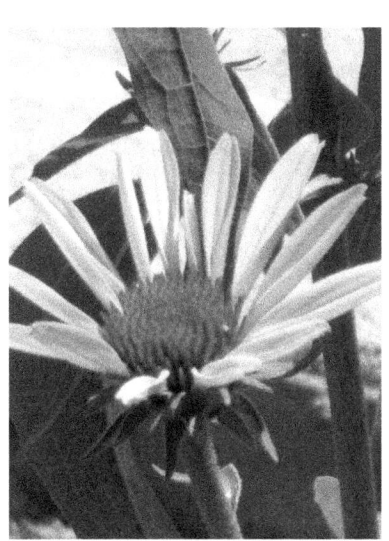

www.ingramcontent.com/pod-product-compliance
Lightning Source LLC
Chambersburg PA
CBHW080833170526

45158CB00009B/2561